2

Middle C

3

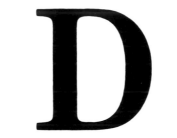

D

7

Middle C

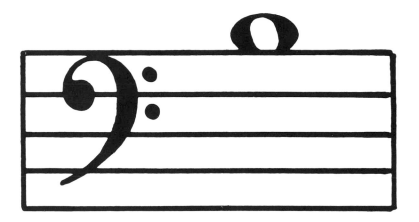

8

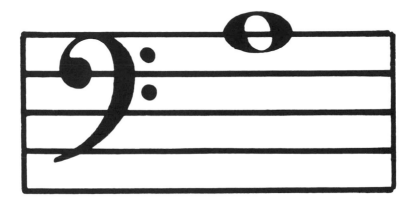

9

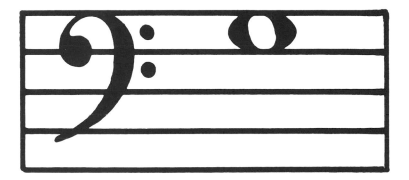

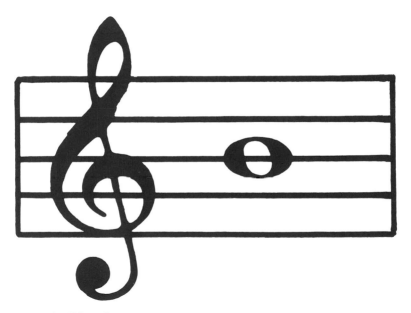

13

16

18

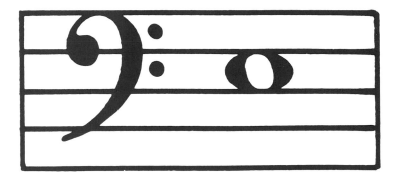

19

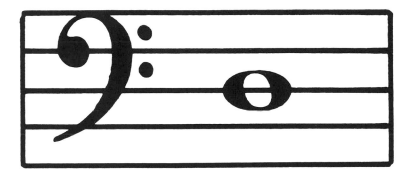

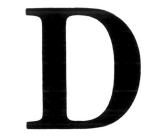

D

 **F** sharp

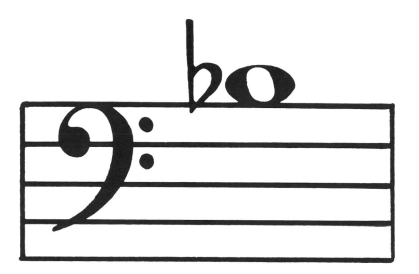

B flat

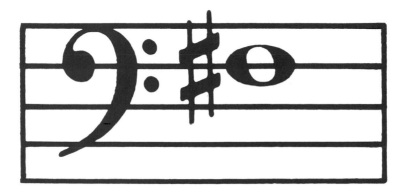

25

F sharp

26

B flat

C sharp

B flat

29

A flat

30

E flat

31

C sharp

E flat

C sharp

A flat

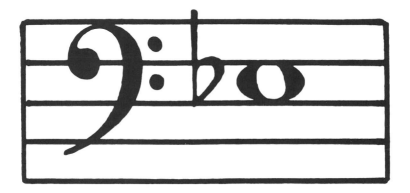

35

E flat

5. MIX AND MATCH (*note values*): Can the pupil match the notes with their value in beats?
For example: $\mathbf{o} = 4$

6. FIND THE TIME (*note values*): Can the pupil find some notes to equal the semibreve in value? For example: ♩ ♩ 𝅗𝅥 = 𝗼

7. RESTING (*rest recognition*): Can the pupil match the rests with their value in beats? For example: 𝄾 = 1 (The following numbers will have matching rests: 4, 4, 3, 3, 2, 2, 1, 1, ½.)

8. CLAP IT OUT (*clap the rhythm*): Peg some cards to a string or board and ask the pupil to clap the rhythm.

9. SET THE PACE (*making rhythms*): The pupil makes up a rhythm, fitting it into a suggested time signature or number of beats. The teacher then claps it.

10. SPELL IT OUT (*spelling*): Can the pupil spell words using the notes? For example: **EGG.**

11. HIGH AND LOW (*octave recognition*): Can the pupil find two or three notes with the same letter-name, and put them in order of low, middle and high?

Enjoy yourselves!

Carol Barratt ♪ ?

IDEAS

1. **NAME THAT NOTE** *(for note recognition)*: Can the pupil name the notes?

2. **LUCKY DIP** *(for fluency of note recognition)*: Put all letter-name cards into a tombola. Ask the pupil to dip a hand in and see how fast the notes can be recognised.

3. **NOTE RACE** *(for fluency of note recognition, and relating notes to the keyboard)*: The teacher/parent puts the letter-name cards into a jumbled pile, with the staves facing up, then turns on a stop-watch as the pupil rushes to pick up a card, goes to the piano and plays it 𝄞 right hand, 𝄢 left hand — but with any finger), shouts out the name and checks it by turning over the card.

4. **COPYCAT** *(theory)*: Can the pupil copy the notes into a manuscript book?

Continued overleaf:

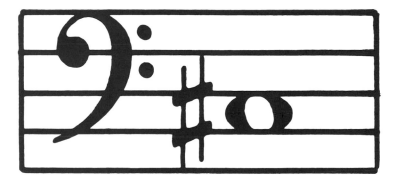

37

C sharp

1/2

41

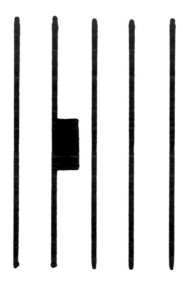

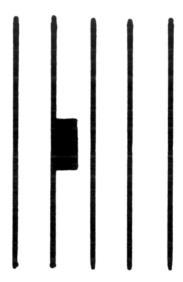

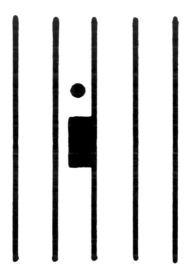

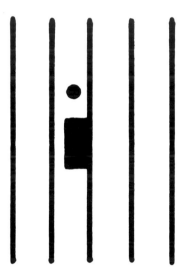

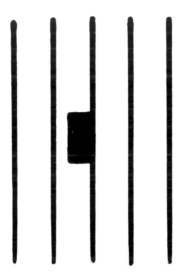

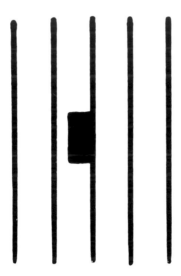

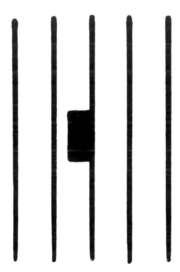

53

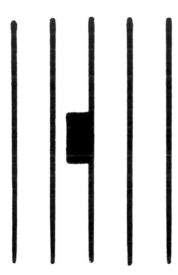

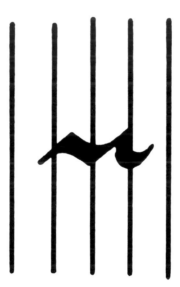

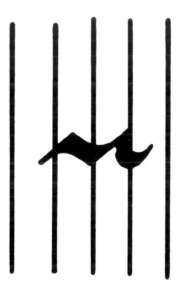

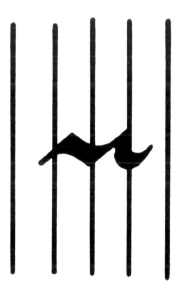

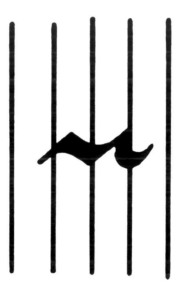

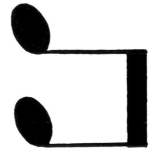

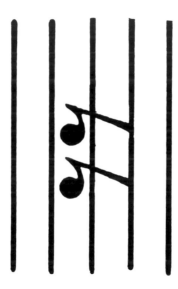

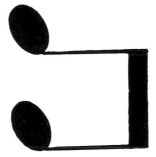

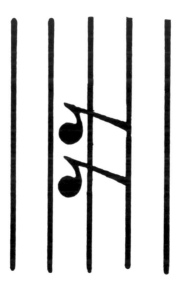

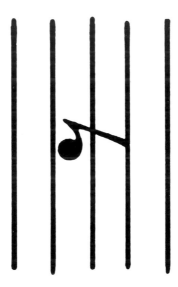

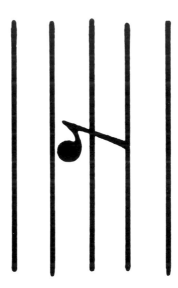

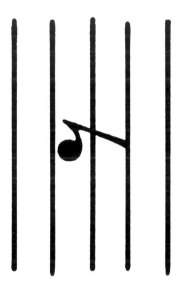

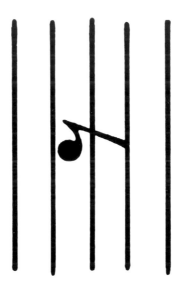

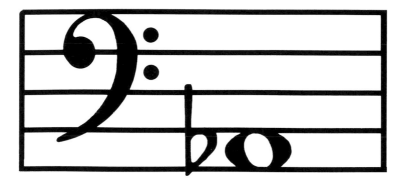

64

A flat

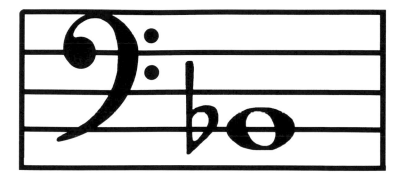

B flat

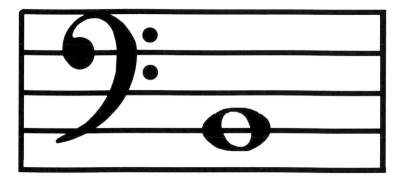

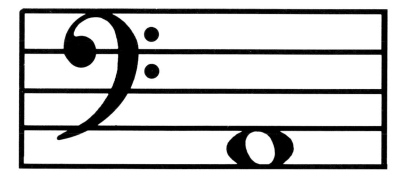

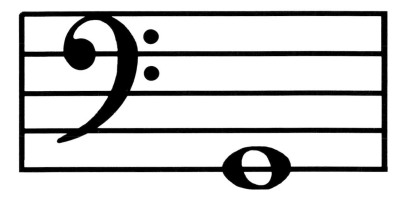

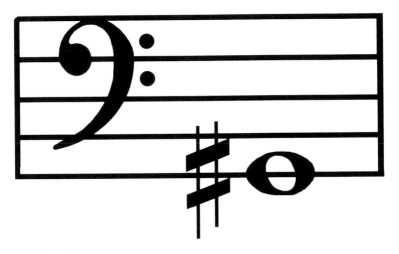

69

G sharp

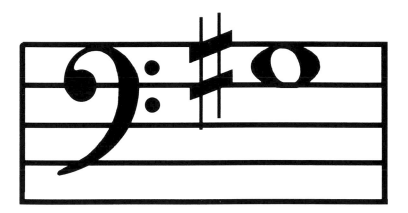

70

G sharp

71

F  sharp